USELESS LANDSCAPE, OR

A Guide for Boys

ALSO BY D. A. POWELL

Tea

Lunch

Cocktails

Chronic

By Myself: An Autobiography
(with David Trinidad)

Repast: Tea, Lunch, and Cocktails

USELESS LANDSCAPE, OR

A Guide for Boys

D. A. POWELL

Graywolf Press

This publication is made possible, in part, by the voters of Minnesota through a Minnesota State Arts Board Operating Support grant, thanks to a legislative appropriation from the arts and cultural heritage fund, and through a grant from the Wells Fargo Foundation Minnesota. Significant support has also been provided by Target, the McKnight Foundation, Amazon.com, and other generous contributions from foundations, corporations, and individuals. To these organizations and individuals we offer our heartfelt thanks.

Published by Graywolf Press
250 Third Avenue North, Suite 600
Minneapolis, Minnesota 55401

www.graywolfpress.org

Published in the United States of America

ISBN 978-1-55597-605-7 (cloth)
ISBN 978-1-55597-695-8

2 4 6 8 9 7 5 3 1
First Graywolf Paperback, 2014

Library of Congress Control Number: 2014935839

Cover design: Kyle G. Hunter

Cover art © Blue Lantern Studio / Corbis

for Ryan

CONTENTS

A Guide for Boys

USELESS LANDSCAPE, OR

A Guide for Boys

Useless Landscape

The beauty of men never disappears
But drives a blue car through the
stars.

—John Wieners

ALMONDS IN BLOOM

In heaven, I believe, even our deaths are forgiven.
—Dunstan Thompson

Who could sustain such pale plentitude
and not want to shake the knopped white blossoms
                from the swarthy branches.

The petals seem more parchment, and more pure,
                in her upright phalanges

with a box of soap flakes, tackling the mud-cake
                somebody made on the quarter-sawn floor.

Just when we think we've been punished enough,
                there's a bounty to contend with—
she's at the spinet, now, and every key's a plunker.
                She hasn't had it tuned since the flood.
Yes, she really troubles heaven with her deaf singing.
                But after all, it's heaven.
                Even death will be forgiven.

TENDER MERCIES

The dandelions, ditch-blown brood,
    the evening snow and dew-soaked phlox,
the Brewer's pea, the Jepson's pea
(these, the bright eyes of the viridian fields)
in chaparral, the hillside pea and angled pea,
        intensities of light and pomp
    that distress the easy upswept grass.
The smack the rain plants as it smudges past
        and penetrates the canvas.

The smattering on field and railroad tracks,
    both hardy blooms and dainty flowers,
the judge's house, the chicken farm,
a migratory camp, a flesh motel,
        a stucco digs
where all that mitigates the August swelter
    is the swamp cooler's immutable burr,
    a straggling house that draws its water
from a hard-water well and flushes out
    with the help of a crude sump pump.

        Before the flatland is occluded
by the staunch of light at end of day,
I wanted to be content with all its surfaces:
        weed, barb, crack, rill, rise . . .
But every candid shoot and fulgent branch
    depends upon the arteries beneath.
The houses have their siphons
        and their circuit vents.
The heart—I mean the literal heart—
must rely upon its own plaqued valves;
the duodenal canal, its unremitting grumble.

              The brain upon its stem,
and underneath,
a network, vast, of nerves that rationalize.

The earth's a little harder than it was.
But I expect that it will soften soon,
        voluptuous in some age hence,
because we captured it as art
                the moment it was most itself:
fragile, flecked with nimbleweed,
                        and so alone,
it almost welcomed its own ravishment.

I was a maiden in this versicolor plain.
        I watched it change.
Withstood that change, the infidelities
of light, the solar interval, the shift of time,
                the shift from farm to town.
I had a man that pressed me down
into the soil. I was that man. I was that town.

They call the chicory "ragged sailors" here:
        sojourners who have finally returned
and are content to see the summer to its end.
        Be unafraid of what the future brings.
I will not use this particular blue again.

                —*for Betty Buckley*

CHERRY BLOSSOMS IN SPRING

I've already pieced it out in my head:
there's almost nothing to go back to.
The wide flat palm of the prickly pear
outside Bent Prop Liquors. I kid you
not that the air's so red, day's end,
that it unlooses a fat ribbon of regret.
Yet the air does not move; it hangs
its squalid rags on the post; it poops
dirty bats out of the public
library's colonnade. I wasn't the first
kid you raped. In this indifferent orchard
where many a shallow boy got dumped.
I think of you often. I think of you never
so much I dare to touch my stolen twig.

THE FLUFFER TALKS OF ETERNITY

I can only give you back what you imagine.
I am a soulless man. When I take you
into my mouth, it is not my mouth. It is
an unlit pit, an aperture opened just enough
in the pinhole camera to capture the shade.

I have caused you to rise up to me, and I
have watched as you rose and waned.
Our times together have been innumerable. Still,
like a Capistrano swallow, you come back.
You understand: I understand you. Understand
each jiggle and tug. Your pudgy, mercurial wad.

I am simply a hand inexhaustible as yours
could never be. You're nevertheless prepared to shoot.
If I could I'd finish you. Be more than just your rag.

LANDSCAPE WITH SECTIONS OF AQUEDUCT

If the crown of day is not gold, then it's a marvelous fake.
Merciful present tense: if the brown grass is always flowing,
if the sun is always just brushing the dry hills, and if
last summer's suicide is still a loner whose white t-shirt
knotted, so tight it had to be cut off his neck with a penknife,
then evening is the same bare patch and the same fat crows,
the crushed aluminum cans and the hamburger wrappers
or the ribbon of tire tread where a road crew hasn't come by.

They have taken him away and I do not know where he is laid.
Among the soft cheat and meadow barley, a live oak begs relief
from the hardened light, the beating of its own gnarled limbs,
and the unrelenting rustle of its own beige blooms that tumble
together shyly like a locker room of boys once boisterous, now
called to roll and suddenly bashful, clasping at dingy towels.
Let the dead be modest. Give the tree, solitary being who feeds
on wind and the mote of another's distant beauty, cause to brag.

Except that the kernel would fall upon the soil, it abides alone.
One guy peeled labels off beer bottles here; another climbed
the remaining concrete piles and wrote JUSTIN LOVES, wrote
STEPHEN LOVES, wrote HANG 'EM HIGH—CLASS OF '93.
Cabbage moths flickered in tansy and clustered broom-rape;
bore the pain of creation for a little yellow dust, a smear of light
on their fidgeting legs and the sudden buoyancy in updraft.
Ruin, by the wayside, you took as sacrament. You, abiding rock.

USELESS LANDSCAPE

A lone cloudburst hijacked the Doppler radar screen, a bandit
hung from the gallows, in rehearsal for the broke-necked man,
damn him, tucked under millet in the potter's plot. Welcome
to disaster's alkaline kiss, its little clearing edged with twigs,
and posted against trespass. Though finite, its fence is endless.

Lugs of prune plums already half-dehydrated. Lugged toward
shelf life and sorry reconstitution in somebody's eggshell kitchen.
If you hear the crop-dust engine whining overhead, mind
the orange windsock's direction, lest you huff its vapor trail.
Scurry if you prefer between the lime-sulphured rows, and cull
from the clods and sticks, the harvest shaker's settling.

The impertinent squalls of one squeezebox vies against another
in ambling pick-ups. The rattle of dice and spoons. The one café
allows a patron to pour from his own bottle. Special: tripe today.
Goat's head soup. Tortoise-shaped egg bread, sugared pink.
The darkness doesn't descend, and then it descends so quickly
it seems to seize you in burly arms. I've been waiting all night
to have this dance. Stay, it says. Haven't touched your drink.

BIDWELL PARK

When the previously withheld faces grew tough as flax
or softened into pliant pine in the umber wood, inclined
together, numerous, when the cobble crushed underfoot,
and pistachios cracked in their shells, grown heavy,
grown consummate among the nibs of leaves, then curious
seemed the stars, those nether eyes which scrutinized
each shape that stirred against the unlit trunks of trees.

He could say he knew the men he did not know. Arrived
in the cedar grove and parted, sated with little effort,
or left unsatisfied, ruminating upon such unfamiliar flesh
across the glade. Silent the approach, a fawn, fluid
through the damp grass, the current in the full creek
surrounding the mossy rocks, pulling them a spell
a little ways downstream, inevitable their deposit.

Thus he would peer the woods, and quarry eluded him,
sloughed that lustrous hide and slipped innominate away.
Retraction: there were times he stood the corsair's nip,
gained midnight's reticent stroke, the haphazard coitus
of loaded collegians stumbling the poison oak. Hermit
thrush or Wilson's snipe. Something bolts the dark,
flushed from the thick rushes, that most temporal cover.

THE KIWI COMES TO GRIDLEY, CA

At first it seems truly foreign, like the downy brown nutsack
in a health class textbook: almost too firm, almost too perfect
to be edible. If it gives to the touch, it's ready to pluck.
No robin's egg, though you might nestle it in your hands.

A few more boys deployed this week. Under jade green vines
they crawl on their crusty elbows, helmets tipped, their
backsides up. And they all went to bliss in their little skiff.

You may never understand the intersection of small & large,
conquest & defeat. For now, miraculous surges simply come,
a series of peaks which are not quite the purple monkshood,
not quite the crusty, papillated surface inside an alien geode.

Consider this odd yield: overgrown berry with its easy sway
and pubescent peel, how it will proffer its redolent fruit.
This mysterious being now enters you: to arms, to arms.

COLLEGE CITY MARKET, COLLEGE CITY, CA

When you come to a fork in the road, you've reached the limit
of inhabited space. That goes for most points on the compass,
leastways true north. And it *is* true, the pavement that splits
the difference, offers you half its lean sandwich, sanderlings,
stink bugs. When you just can't drive: offers you a pallet.

The register sticks. The swatter will not nearly vanquish its prey.
Bursts its lid in geyser spray, a jar of pickled pork rinds.
Eats its way through tin, the green chile salsa called *verde*.
Dies one afternoon, the rat who had nibbled too much cereal;
and, though his location is vague, you can smell him decay,
up through floorboards wafting. Light a candle then blow it out.
When a customer wrinkles his nose, just look the other way.

Grasshoppers pitch themselves against the wire front door.
Nothing in the cooler they desire. They don't want flan or beer.

SEVEN SKETCHES FOR A LANDSCAPE, UNFINISHED

1

The state, begun as a series of missions,
      used native men & women as cheap labor,
edified through occasional public floggings.
      As the indigenous populations began to die,
they were replaced by immigrants from China
           used to build railroads,
      with pickaxes and blasting caps.
And when the Chinese were too many,
      the US Congress passed exclusion acts.

2

In Wheatland, hops pickers, fired upon
      by Yuba County sheriffs and their henchmen
           for attempting to protect themselves
against exploitation and unsafe working conditions,
      retaliated by rioting; were beaten and cuffed.

3

In Cocoran, the Mexican strikers were refused relief.
      Some infants starved. Some workers died.
The farmers dumped their milk into the sewers,
           and burned acres of corn, rather
      than provide for upstart laborers.

4

Old man Nakagawa, divested of his property in 1942,
returned to Marysville following the war
and opened a small grocery.

5

While then-governor Ronald Reagan
stood in the capitol's rose garden,
members of the Black Panther Party for Self-Defense
entered the senate chambers,
armed to protect their community
from the abuse of power exhibited by Oakland police.

6

When the Islamic mosque on Tierra Buena Road
was set ablaze by arsonists,
the neighboring Sikhs opened up their temple
as a place of worship
for their historic enemies.

7

The rains still bring the rivers to a crest.

[Here's where you imagine the rest.]

A BRIEF HISTORY OF INTERNMENT

Hence the wild daikon.
We've made the landscape mean here.
And then we put down roots.

THE BATHERS

What a reprieve from all this stultifying heat.
And all the threats implicit in that heat:

the sweep and snare of blackberry,

razor barb of concertina wire.

The bluish teasel nearly chafed you
with its bracts.

You've made it through some muck
with your absolute body
still intact. So far,

the Camp Far West lakewater is barely blue.
That might make two of you.

Who is the other whom you seek?

They found a body in this lake; it wasn't his;
it wasn't yours. And so the shore
persists in summoning you.

He may be waiting.
His body hasn't lost any allure.
& nor has yours.

But sorry is the heart
that knows
what's round the bend.

LITTLE BOY BLUE

He finds himself inside the Sunrise Mall,
but not at Waldenbooks. He seeks no solitude.
His second great awakening has started,
subdued interstices between kiosks and stores;
the proximity of skimming eyes, or studious eyes
that read him like a copy of *Leaves of Grass*.
He has come in his holey, worn-out jeans.
He has come there in his flimsy little thongs.

And there's those hankering eyes that seem
to sample him like Orange Julius eggwhite froth
or bits of free salami cubed upon a paper plate
& stabbed by frill-picks.
                    Don't meet those eyes.
The arcade's packed with Pac-Man players in a jiff.
Gobble the cherries. Gobble that consecrated ghost.

DYING IN THE DEVELOPMENT

Sometimes the odd half acre with a precipitous grade
      can be remedied with a dry-laid retaining wall
instead of having to backhoe cut and fill.

Finding ways to stop erosion should be easy
      before partition, before the open slope's divided.

Such is the innocuous nature of topography,
before the Whatzits move in with their impudent kid,
the Doughboy pool depreciates the terrace's integrity
      or, down the street, a Taco Bell and KFC
merge as one fantastical beast with crispy wings.

We shall not all sleep but we shall all be changed.

I think the awful family's name was actually White.
      I did the sleepover there: burn-outs in black tees,
their bodies beginning to prosper, pelotage whorled out
into dark cowlicks, mildly offensive-smelling flowers
      bunched in the night, then untucking as we rose
to the morning's listless mother, the fest of sausages
      and toaster waffles, milk moustaches,
"the carton says *homo*," "*homo?* sick," and belching.
          Just don't serve me no Tang, I thought.
            I hated the taste of Tang.

Unsurprising what gets blocked out, reapportioned.
      I say it was a rustic place, but in transition.
I say the land was sculpted,
      but it was simply held back. "Held back,"
said of the White boy. Denied promotion to the tenth.

And as the grade remained the same, he worsened.
Continuation school. Vocational Ed. Juvenile detention.

      The property values rose slightly; then depreciated.
The retaining walls declined in their integrity.
Not the fault of anyone, really. It was a lean half acre.

      It was a mean development, no outlet,
no opportunity, except the kind that came tooling
up the street in a Vega, playing Ecstasy Passion & Pain.

I realize this might read solely as an allegory:
      the peregrines that hovered there,
the Mormons and recruiters and the suck-ass school,
Vice-Principal Pervy who would paddle young behinds.
      But that's not only striped resurfacing.
It's the entire slipshod construction: a site where
           everything happened gradually;
it was so gradual, it was practically overnight.

CHICKEN

The metallic taste I got from being served upon a tray
      in the Sac County Jail, or bumped against
the dented cans at the Dented Can Warehouse.
The stale scent, the elbow scrapes: I was a billiard ball
for those who cared to knock me in the pockets
on the table in The Wreck Room afterhours.
It wasn't only Amtrak pulling trains each night.
Each man who lost his stake in me had lost
      his gamecock, his bathhouse boychick,
the pullet at the pumphouse, the tipsy one, free-living.

The cues were often skewed. When simple coxcombs
      preened, I wasn't squeamish on their knees
as, without means, I groomed their inch-long wattles.
I'm getting on in years. I'm past my freshness date.
If I have balked at play, it's that this chicken
      tastes no more like table fowl. I blame the microwaves.
You blame the chemicals and drugs. Yes, I'm a little overdone,
I'll warrant you. You want a little cut. Get in here, then,
      pull back the skin and crisp it,

before the insatiate drunks come round with greasy fingers,
distribute me between the bars, and pinch my biscuits.

BOJANGLES

You've gone and gotten cozy with the doorman;
        he's so smitten, he's ready to lose his job.
How did you get here, he wants to know.
You go all kitten in his lap. You're almost genuine.
Once you're in, who cares if you've blown your cover.

You've got to put on the outfit that says:
        I don't want to fuck you. I just want to dance.
But also: meet me in the parking lot with some blow.
                To the outskirts of Tooterville you go—
(nobody holds a gun to your head.
Nobody beats you with a length of hose.
        You're cute when you're young and cute.
Now wipe those lips. Now wipe that runny nose.)
        —with a little white slut.

DYING IN A TURKISH BATH

Remind me to tell you about the sculpted figures
an eye can devour, the imperfect laws of gravity
and the imperfect ceiling, the hot stone floors.

Someone's pressing against me in the steam, again.
I want to make sure it's you who's ravishing
in the lead-white pools, the salty declivities.

I expect we'll both harden like old bread. I expect
we'll have seen each hoodlum and attendant
to the point we'll naturally shrink away. We will

have had so many good figs and the green grapes.
So much soap, we'll have stung our tender openings.
Bearing against one another, in the opaque spray.

END OF DAYS

I have seen a hawk owl's shadow across the street.

That doesn't mean that I have seen a hawk owl.

He could join with me in the perfect guise of a bird.

Wild forms are with us always, though fleeting.

There are no particular things to make me love anyone,
least of all, not you.

On the wings of that great speckled bird.

THAT'S WHERE THEY HIDE THE SILOS

Did the vast slope bear flax
and cheat all summer?
Fill me in. I haven't the heart
to make myself a study in the grass.

Unlikely to climb the broad stone fences.
Unlikely to improve. Fodder easily gained
might not provide for—us, ungainly quail.

Proceed toward the blinds.
You'll hear the report, later.
You'll think, just take your limit
this time, you'll think
the failsafe dawn breaks
soon enough
and treacherous is the road.

PANIC IN THE YEAR ZERO

Bless the tourists in their "Alcatraz Rocks!" parkas
     on the upper deck of a double-decker
          in any given February bluster.
They could have sworn it would be warm here,
     just because the cryometer says it isn't cold.

Who the hell would look at a cryometer?
     People from arctic regions, I suppose.

People who must have flown in over the map's flat face;
     who must have seen the latest developments;
          the delta's brackish mouth; windmills
waving white banderoles against the crisping brown hills.
     Spring looks a lot like summer looks a lot
          like drought. What would anyone expect
if they knew the way planarity invites the opportunist.
     Aren't the dispatches the same, reaching them
in Chehalis, Waterloo and Asbury Park. Even
if folks don't watch what passes now for news,
          I assume they go to cocktail parties.
          Or they Twitter.
They don't all have snug jammies and Ovaltine,
     though they seem to get snugger by the minute.
What kind of help could they get if they could get help?
          Help them make this dull show seem like art.
     Help the supporting cast appear
in the end, summoned from the cities of the plain,
     and appear to end and end again
          as in a wide shot of the Battle of the Marne.
Be tolerant of those you cannot seem to understand.
          And other such advice.

It's the quiet part of the morning service,
    while I'm writing this down:
Thank God for the quiet part.

And thank God for the one who held me to my wickedness;
    who asked me to revel in it,
            even though it cost us both a little dignity.
It's easy for me to look back at what's destroyed.
I knew it would be destroyed, like a wicked town.
I never thought "that town is where the heart is."
I simply thought "that town is where the town is."
Usually someplace inhospitable, and filled with
    handsome men. The kind who kill you
with their handsomeness, or their acute cordage.

Hell is the most miraculous invention of love,
            no matter how the love turns out.
Hell is the place from whence the music of longing—
which accounts for most of what we call music—
    gets written.

I'm tired of this idea of hell, no matter how functional.
    Sure, I've had my petty doubts.
Like the extra pills I've stashed in my Eva Braun box,
    waiting for the bomb to hit Bakersfield,
        or some other place in the near distance
(this plan only works if there's some kind of distance)
        the sign that it's time to pull up stakes,
head for those durable hills with my pemmican,
    my Port-o-pot, my jerry cans,
        and yes, I too would have Ovaltine.

Though I guess it would be made with water
                    instead of milk.
Such would be the dark days
            if we think the dark days really must come.

But I have lived through perilous times,
            and I do not love them.
I cannot pretend I'm smart about such things.
I mean: look at the sloppy slew I've been.
            And you were there. And you.
You've seen me rumple down the sidewalk like a moocher.
Lord knows, you've seen me hit that sidewalk on my keister.

            "Scandalous," the tourists said,
                    and flashed.
And when the worst of the drama came,
            they clucked their tongues and threw their change.
Something inside each one of us is cocked
            like the ear of a hound,
and half the time we hunt, and half the time we rescue,
            because we're never really sure
                    if the humans will beat us or feed us.
If we are our better selves, it's just a wonder.
And if we're not.

            Even in our legends, angels come.
They try their best. But we're such shits.
            And it's not because we want to screw them.
We screw *everything*. We're mankind. It's what we do.
I've probably sullied a few white wings myself.

That's not the problem.
So much has passed between us, we're practically cousins.
The problem is, we're so bent on an ending,
              we'll sunder the entire valley,
with conviction. With an invented coda of immunity.
Nobody in this picture is granted immunity.
              If it were available, I'd have gotten it for myself.

              Enough with the apocalypse, already.
Think of all the history you've read. It started somewhere.
              It started at absolute zero, is what you thought.
Just because you couldn't know what came before.
              But imagine: something did.

LANDSCAPE WITH TEMPLE, MOSQUE AND LITTLE CROSSES

How, even if you broke an oath—slandered your god
in the long summer months, when friends were generous
and a winking man in a linen shirt bought breakfast—

you, taking what you could from one man's ice chest,
another's burgeoning walnut groves, a lady's purse
left open on her chair (she'd gone to check her lips)—

how you'd be welcomed into unexpected corridors:
manifold, the curves and dimples in the service road,
which—if you waited—had this way of evening out.

Take nothing with you now. Distrust that atlas.
You tried to be all things to others, too. It didn't work.
The byways narrowed. Soft shoulders caved. You can't

expect a rescue from such an ingress all the time.
Emergency service ends. You cross the county line.

LANDSCAPE WITH COMBINE

My father's fields are far from here.
I shot my share of blackbirds there.
Drove a harvester in summer.
Gathered plums.
Gathered chums.
The tractor-trailer rigs would come.
The pickers, singularly or in vans.
And in summer the canneries began.

If I was asked to ride the John Deere then.
To reap, I'd reap; to thresh, I'd thresh. Men,
I'd winnow you. I'd winnow a few.
I'd take you, dear John, or whoever is you.
Love is easier to achieve than you might think. Sooner
or later the combine gives out. & sooner.

QUARANTINE

Sounds like a miner's melody. Or a gemstone set in platinum.
A set of blonde and imbricated petals. The perplexing swish
of botany's haste. A season originates, then gratifies and ends.
Sounds like so many things that happen as *beyond*.

Now entering. Solve all arboreal problems that you can.
Then what to do when boxelder bugs aren't rampant:
that's a different set of worries. Play worry in different keys.
C is where you always start and end. Or so my teacher said.

For he was taken by the logic of the dominating swarm,
the way it left the punctured globes upon the boughs.
We played a spray of ditties in his wake. They sounded like

most pickers (those in tempo; those articulating their misfortunes).
Or at least that's what I imagined going on. Black dots spread,
black spots. Pretty soon the world is one great gall. Then what?
Then we hide in the meadow. Oh, how it hums, this meadow.

RELEASE THE STERILE MOTHS

The flutter, apple brown, invites
      a certain scientific approach
we just ain't nailed down yet.

We bamboozle these little peacherinos
      by dispersing infertile mates, some
of whom in turn will flimflam the dickens
      out of prospective progenitors.

Every unpleasant bug deserves his day
      with the bunco artist rendition
of himself. Why shouldn't it end there?
      The barbarous insect ultimately

brought down with federal grants
      and pheromones. But always
another invader tends to come. Just ask
      the avocado commission.

Just ask the woodbine to show you
      where the varmints hide,
waiting to punk you in the plums.

VALLEY OF THE DOLLS

9 o'clock. Time to smoke a joint
        that lets me take my pills.

10 o'clock. Time to take my pill
        to take my pills.

11 o'clock. I take my pills.

12 o'clock. I take my little pills.

I call them dolls this time.
        I take my dolls.

I always loved this film.
        But then: I wasn't in it.

When did I stop feeling sure, feeling
        safe, and start wondering why

Suspense, you're killing me.
        [close-up on dolls]

LANDSCAPE WITH FIGURES PARTIALLY ERASED

First, it's just the faces disappearing.
Because, deflected, as the faces long have been,
with their hunched trunks
and mercilessly twisted necks,
they can only be regarded from a ground's-eye view.

The bellwort tips its fallow head down
in the hot tomato field. The green snake rests
beneath the green leaves, and the air is toast.
Diesel tractors grind to the frontage and idle there,
their heads bowed, too, like giant wooden horses
meant to sack an unsuspecting city.
Down come the earthen walls.

My father used to pour libations onto the ground
from the gas pump's nozzle, and I'd swirl
its iridescence, respire it into my lung's core,
so woozy, so sick, and awed by the vapors.
Fire beguiled me, too. As did the concept of force.

Whole villages burned in a single spritz.
Even now the past gets altered. We forget
because our friends won't suffer that subject again.
Because the students tap their pens uncomfortably,
look around to see if anyone else is taken in.
That's when we figure it's best to make a joke.

I've wandered, now, from the corrugated sheds,
with people half in and half out of nuclear range.
My retention of the facts is not a silo.
Even if it were, some disrepair gets fallen into.
I like to think we dismantle thought
as much as tortuous thought dismantles us.

I have seen sharp men lose limbs. Women too.
A hand pulled off, conveyed into the hopper.
But these were country matters.
Like frilled silhouettes of flowering wild carrot,
white against the mackerel white sky,
the texture is imperishable, the details

so far off. These bodies: their contours
uncertain. Just a general cast to the light.

HOMESICKNESS

There were others I'd forgotten, who,
without vocabularies
      to commend them to my broken landscapes,
           went missing
throughout the daylight hours, then struck
      their faint electric jags
upon the silhouettes of water birches.
What is he doing there along the bypass?
      Or that one, thumbing up into the hills.
         Spikelets.
      The field and the fire devoured them.

I don't drive, nor return, nor conclude.
I wouldn't know now the etiquette
      of being in someone else's car,
much less someone's memory.
      How do they stand it, these apparitions.
Summoned from the nude buckwheat
      with blatant inaccuracy
then dispatched with a gesundheit blink.
He could have taken the train.
He could have just decided he'd rather walk.

He was an EMT who owned a pinball machine.
      He was the jeweler's son.
         Carried hardly any cash.
      He was a fragment friend, that one.
I only saw him after hours.
      From Dunnigan. Woodland. Galt. Esparto.
Recollection isn't mine to master.

Worse than all the figures I could choose,
             the gangly birds.
They are the heedless shapes we come upon
        suddenly, and without warning,
                their dun quills overstating

that final moment of distress.
        And then the scattering.
        And then the progress,
which is always away.
Where did that one go?
He went away.
            Away now, then,
my feathered friend. You are not now,
nor have you ever been.

BUGCATCHING AT TWILIGHT

A round yellow fury to the evening's light,
though ultimately it shows clemency. Shadow,

you put out your gentian-lipped goblet
and the night's lost sailors bumbled in,
a whole handful of them, squeezed into
those snug white pants.

Sorry. I mean
those were meadowhawk's wings.

You long for places you shouldn't go:
billiard halls, the pachinko palace,
behind the parked car where a Zippo flicks,
twice (sometimes you need to be summoned
twice), the places where no neon glows.

(And the *you* here is not so much you as it is I.)

I have this rearrangement to make:
symbolic death, my backward glance.
The way the past is a kind of future
leaning against the sporty hood.
On leave, he says.
He doesn't say it, but you can see it:
flattop, civvies, shirt tucked too neat.
He is so at ease, you think. You think: *at ease.*

You only have between now and o-dark-thirty.

The swift birds amass.
They, too, drawn to the buzz
hanging on the cusp of dusk.

HEAD OUT ON THE HIGHWAY

The search for a likely place to pull over
gets more difficult each day,
as cloverleaf and cloverleaf give way
to fast food exits and unlikely outlets.

We get better at doing something,
so we do it every day. Every day,
we do the something, even if it kills us.
Which it does.

There's nothing at the package store
that we can't get on the internet.
And it's not like the price of gas
goes down. Nor anything else.

I've been wanting a lonely lane
that's off the map. I need to stretch.
And if you want to neck, we'll neck.
As long as I can get out; take a leak.

Frog bodies spread like throw rugs
across the blacktop. So enticing—
were we small enough—to cuddle there.
But everybody's small in a Pontiac.

Or rather, no one ever is too big.

TARNISHED ANGEL

Though they're slightly eroded, one still might surmise
the commanding force in those tensile coppery legs,
their responsive bent, their brutal extent. I draw up
into myself at their coming; I stumble as one cast out.

Look down on me. I, fallen, would meet him, fallen,
in the blunt blue light of morning. My angry god
would contest his angry god, to clutch at sheer cloth
and recompense of lean, fusible flesh. Once lost wax.

I long to know his vulgar tongue. To feel the cool verdigris
of his shanks, the clasping down upon my own extremities.
I want to be with the one who will not have me. Will not,
despite our mortal errors, which seem terribly to twin.

RIVERFRONT PARK, MARYSVILLE, CA

Half the year, all we smell is the sewage treatment plant,
down near the boat launch ramp.

And all we hear is the chug of bass boats idling in,
the slide of the hitch pin.

The black-coated dog swims and shakes himself dry. He is
rid of fleas, which weren't his.

Would that we could rid ourselves of everything not ours:
reverse the birthing hour,

return the beastings to their teats; jizz to its bushed nub.
Cars circle here at night—

They flash their lights at someone in the outhouse shadow
or pass like slinking cats

afraid to taste the stranger's milk. It's okay, my dear.
Someone cares for you here.

Were you dying, here's a fine place for your mangy head.
Hush. Someone's backing in.

LOVE HANGOVER

Old Tricks Mix

I could not tell you then who actually was attractive.

I'd blow the devil if he offered. Apparently he did.

& neither can I tell you anymore what goes together.

Love, as a song, is sorry enough, without its equally sorry singer.
Love, when it's truly sorry, is sorrier than a broke-dick dog.

LANDSCAPE WITH LYMPHATIC SYSTEM, SYSTEM OF RIVULETS, SYSTEM OF RIVERS

My body, when did you amble down
        from the levee, begin to wade

with no bead head midgefly or green glitter jig
to flick, quick winglet, at the end of translucent line

nor noontime college bake party
        along the weed-slumped banks

                nor the tiretube, tame-water floating.

      Nor encounter with same vivid weekday man
previously unknown to you, and unknown still.
Stepped down to you, into the water with you,
parted you, transfigured you said leave me alone
said punish me I am an unrepentant boy.

          You are not that body now.

Wherever you were headed was not this stream.

Your asscheeks sag. Your abdomen distends.
        Nothing has a tight hold on your guts.
Guts spill at times when they're not tucked away.

Winded, white-haired body. Splotchy skin.
        A face uneven as a river jag
and asperous as the mullein's flannel leaves.

My undesirable body, you're all I have to fiddle with.
The fiddle's wood has cracked but it still plays.
The music, rival falls into the eddy, into brisk cascade
        and latterly to rest on strand exhausted.
You are the form of my exhaustion as you break.

Tenderness in the testes, tenderness of mind.
        I have come to admire you in the water.
You are the yellow crown of some narcissus afterward:
        the fizzled salvo. The burst of yolk
that has begun to dry on the stoneware plate.
The mess. A young Picasso's stab at fingerpaints
hung and fading on his mom's refrigerator door.
        But not without a certain coruscating charm.

        You are run-off from the melting foothills,
with your specks of gold. Mostly pyrite,
        though that captivates as well.
We need those flecks to break the river's surface,
        its decided syntax. I need you to come down
from the sunflowered shore. Unexpected oxbow.
Unexpected age. You are an engineering failure.
        I'm your systemic glitch.

Here, where the shallows pool up into habitus,
        I behold the imperfection of you, my mass,
my faulted body. Despite the plunging falls
        with you, I swim.

AN ELEGY FOR MY LIBIDO

Well, here it is, the Oscar race has started
  and there isn't a single movie
    I'm dying to see.

What ever did I like about the winter?
  There was the taste of candied yams—
    but all that *sugar.*

The other day a young man on the bus
  offered me his seat.
    I was quick to take it.

Meaning that, as I sat,
  his rear filled my horizon
    like a khaki-colored sun.

I've had a profusion of dawns
  in every Abercrombie hue.
    Catalogues? Frankly, catalogues

are a goddamned waste.
  The better I felt,
    the quicker he moved away.

ABANDONMENT UNDER THE WALNUT TREE

"Your gang's done gone away."
—The 119th Calypso, *Cat's Cradle,*
Kurt Vonnegut, Jr.

Something seems to have gnawed that walnut leaf.

You face your wrinkles, daily, in the mirror.
But the wrinkles are so slimming, they rather flatter.

Revel in the squat luck of that unhappy tree,
who can't take a mate from among the oaks or gums.

Ah, but if I could I would, the mirror version says,
because he speaks to you. He is your truer self
all dopey in the glass. He wouldn't stand alone
for hours, without at least a feel for the gall of oaks,
the gum tree bud caps, the sweet gum's prickly balls.

Oh, he's a caution, that reflection man.
He's made himself a study in the trees.
You is a strewn shattered leaf I'd step upon, he says.
Do whatever it is you'd like to do. Be quick.

THE PRICE OF FUNK IN FUNKYTOWN

Because I have no sense
          and I like the way it sounds:
     if I was to buy me a little place,
I'd buy me some bottomland.

The reason that the bus is always stopping here
     is that it used to stop here.
Nothing's bound to change until we make it change.

"I'll get off when I want," the gentleman announces.
     "I'm getting very old. Besides,
          I'm leaving."

okay, stop me if you've heard this one . . .

TRAVELING LIGHT

about the yellow flowers of the flannelbush,
      those little Danish cookies made of butter.

I mustn't tarry. The snails that feed here
just might consume me. And why wouldn't they?

I have known them occasionally to hustle
for a chance to slurp away the dreamy stars.

Q: how do you ruin any good trick?
      A: you fatten him up.

If I can't have my health, at least I'll have my humor.
    Good Humor. Here come the icecream man.

A Guide For Boys

And no one goes back to his God unscathed.

—Nelly Sachs

OUTSIDE THERMALITO

Persimmons ripen with the first frost.
            The bitterness inflicted on them
                       takes their bitterness away.

Would that there were some other way.

THE OPENING OF THE COSMOS

You'd have thought me a blushed newbie, to look at my face then.
        And you'd have been wrong.
Discolored, yes. But that was an accident on the pommel horse.
        That was the beating I took from the wind,
                trying to work my way uptown.

If I retracted, I'd retract just like the milksnake's scarlet skin:
        welcome to the past. Here is my private self to greet you.
I am the spitting image of the night's prehensile lips,
ready to clamp you against the solid surface of my palate.
And I am the new sap, aroused by spring, the hard xylem,
the knotty stick whose protuberance sends forth new shoots.
                Didn't you say you always wanted a child?
I can be that too: the whippersnapper who follows you.
        Or maybe you want the youth who'll do your labors
and be paid in what little kindness you can manage.

        Go back and try to snag me while I'm yet unspoilt.
The morning's saporous dew, the early strut of the cockerel,
        the first fugitive act of copulation, which,
                because it is a first, feels like a last.
You picked it all when you picked me out:
what satisfied you, what couldn't love you back.

The endless act of revising. And with that, the revision.

ONE THOUSAND AND ONE NIGHTS

& afterwards.
The carnal is one type of aesthetic display
a little hamlet can suffer through.

Along with all the body's meta-meta-metaphors,
from transients to the Department of Public Health.

There are so many reasons I'm not there.
So many reasons to let that lazy sentence
stand as substitute for work I should want to do.

I should want to toil those imaginary fields.

For they *are* imaginary fields, many, by now.
That's where a good deal of the tension lies.
All fields catch fire.
That's not so dire.

I got to be the toast of C Street
for a while, the bee of The Beehive on B Street.
There was no A to speak of.

Besides.
It was a B kind of town, wasn't it?

An exhibition to celebrate the humble prune.
Six stories high, the grand hotel.
That's the gamut, dammit.

Minus the gore. I had to spare you the gore.
How else could I lead you this far,
except to pretend that nothing perishes, especially
matters that disturb the heart.
Ah, the heart . . .

What is the heart but a boob, anyways,
that it should hang out at the rodeo arena,
long after the bulls have been roped.

FUNKYTOWN: FORGOTTEN CITY OF THE PLAIN

I wanted to be either the first man, unashamed of his nakedness,
        or the angel sent down to test the will of man.
Take my scrawny youth, the mischief I made, the way

        I faced my God down daily. He made me a slab of clay,
and I could be molded, kneaded, pushed through a Fun Factory™.
I gave myself to a lot of men. It was okay. I was okay. & them.

It happened when the canneries shut down.
                The vats were finally hosed, the pressure valves
turned off and rolls of unused labels got warehoused.

        That's when the fellows packed it in.
And discontent was discontent to the power of ten.
        Because I was a minor then, my record's sealed.

Besides, who would want to know my shady ways,
        except projectionists who caught me in their beams,
the lanky escapees who worked the dime toss at the fair,

                or pulled the saddle ponies,
demonstrated the strongest knife. Who made their way
to the wood that constellated the valley. Oh, the many,

        many balls a single man could juggle then.
And I would ask "are you my angel?" (I got that from a book)
((I was so unoriginal. They called me "Unoriginal Sin"))

        The humor of it all fell flat. Humor does that.
S.O.S./Fire in the Sky and *Funkytown*. The rapture happened.
        Exactly who most people wouldn't expect:

I'd rather withhold names. Besides, you'd read the entire list
                    and never know the sass and grace of them.
Ladies from the D Street storefronts, boys from fields,
the pickers, gleaners, lifters, lumpers, men who shot cogged dice,
women on foodstamps, kids who got blown, who were blown to bits,
the wizened gents, dramatic boys who *knew a man Bojangles*

and they'd dance a lick. The quarterback. Somebody's ex.

As long as there is room, why not let all the people in?
                    There'd be no heartache then.

        We will outlast this time, my friends.

When I am taken o when I am taken o when I am taken

NOTES OF A NATIVE SON

I'm the truest sort of resident. The kind who,
asked to offer proof that he resides here, fails.
The guy who comes from someplace else & thrives
better than fremontodendron or another local shrub.

I am the child of Argonauts. I'm that Ithaca man
who's been pre-ordained to wander
just like a common fieldhand, a vacher.
Lotus eaters tempt him.

Sorcery. Seduction. With your permission,
I'm going to make a lot of this story up.
Here is California, region of new mythologies,
the substitute for plot: a history pageant

covering every prospect of the valley
and its processions, from the tardy Donner Party
to the efficiency of the Overnite Express.
That was some caravan.

I slept a long time in the backseat of the car.
Which worked out well for me. For I knew little else.
Except to keep expectations low and myself high.
Who wants to go to Lodi? So do I. So do I.

DONKEY BASKETBALL DIARIES

The rules are fairly similar.
                    Dribble before you shoot.
Touch your own foolish beast at all times,
even as you covet the strong asses of others.

Don't expect to remain impeccable
                    in this gymnasium—

incarnate, after all, you certainly might slip
                    a bit
especially where there's shit on the floor.
Frankly, these planks are prosperous in shit.

You are an unrepentant wretch
            from the moment that you tip off
                    to each moment that you score.
Go on and beat this dumb animal
            if it drives him down the court.
            That's the type of player you've become.
Even though it's scrimmage.
                    And novelty scrimmage at that.
The crowd came out to see you at your worst.

Get to the top of the key first.

My Saturday athlete, the donkey is braying.
Let me lift you into some triumphant dream,
            wherein we're entering the gate of a city.

Before I toss you into the warm brown loaves,
let me carry you toward that celestial hoop
                    if only for a few cloddish steps.

Were we fully able to enjoy each other's agony
I'm afraid it wouldn't be very much of a game.

A LITTLE LESS KETTLEDRUM, PLEASE

The field commander, in his regal busby,
        tosses his corded mace into the air.
He, too, excites the eye. Just as the color guard,
        those shako hats and twirling sabres,
            trot out our choreographed
tribute to something. The Hundred Years' War?

Boom shaka-lacka lacka, boom shaka-lacka lacka,
        I'm part of a fantail movement
stepping time in the eye of a peacock feather.
            Hear me, up there in the bleachers?
I may be the least of all the piccolos.
But mine's the tune you'll whistle as you leave.

Now have all the mosquito trucks come by
            to prepare the grounds.
And now has the unnatural grass
        been freshly mowed and limed.
            The drumline has reviewed all day
wheeling a battery of tympani without a glitch.

If you heard a chirping flycatcher out of place,
        that was not me. It was the reeds.
For I save all my wind to expend uptempo
        on *Close Encounters of the Third Kind Theme*
by the maestro, Mr. John Williams.
           We do a scramble pattern then.

That's when I imagine I am to be struck
      by the first trombone, like a turgid wet wiener
        thumping my shower bum
  when coach averts his supervisory gaze.
Or, abject under the walnut tree,
      he'll make me practice the *Overture to Tommy*.

A junior who slides through valves like that,
      who works the phrase with such aplomb,
will surely be able to play me something
        from the Great American Songbook,
be it *Body & Soul* or *Jelly Jelly*. Anything will do.
    Except *I Can't Get Started with You*.

    & just for the record I'll have you know
        I play on the football team, too.
I just don't play on all of them at once.

NARCISSUS

Not every boy who desires fame gets it the way he wants.
Not every flower, leaning vainly toward his own face
reflected in a murky puddle, gets to meditate upon himself
more than a few transitory days, before he, too, molders.

You should have stayed wild in some valley town
if that's the life you wanted. You can't have it now.
Too many people know you as the affable but obvious
mussy downtown hussy. Blown limp by any passing wind.

MY LIFE AS A DOG

If I was a dog, the only three things I'd chase:
    a firetruck, a ball, and my own tail.
If I was a dog, you wouldn't be petting me
    I might have rolled in something.

As a dog, I'd roll over for cheese. Not very good cheese.

I'd bark all night until you let me out.
    You'd have to let me out.
Don't worry, I wouldn't chase anyone's cat.
I'm sure I'd think about it. But I just wouldn't.

Someone would have to hold me when I got my shots.
    Would you hold me when I got my shots?

I'd sneak into the garden and eat the pears off the trees.
How would I do that? I'd be a dog. A crafty dog.

If I was a dog, I'd have run away by now.
    I'd be a runaway. You'd think *bad dog*.

And when it was time to put me down, you'd be
    a little blue. Then put me down.

A GUIDE FOR BOYS

The first knot doesn't count.
You're bound to fuck it up.
The rabbit comes out of the hole;
he starts to circle the tree. Halfway home,
he finds another bunny. So they tangle.

To build a fire without a match,
locate a woody-tissued branch
that's light in lignin.
Also something to cause friction. You
may need to ask a pal for his assistance.
You might need to use
somebody's shirt to catch the sparks.

Now you're ready for the lean-to.

Now you're ready for the closeness
of a makeshift bunk and shelter.

And in the night you make your meal
of foraged mushrooms.
Careful, friend. The edible ones,
with their sublime aroma of earth,
are what you're after. Not the snowy,
bulbous caps of amanitas, no matter
how much they entice you.

Nuts are always nice,
though they may need grinding.
Try acorns, shagbark hickories,
piñon pine, or burry chestnuts.

Roast the flowerheads of cattails;
make a salad of their shoots.

In the woody honeysuckle vine,
you may find robins' eggs. If so,
you might try roasting them in clay.

And why not devise a language
while the bonfire dims. The camp's
a temporary site, you say, using
Navajo Code Talkers' tongue.

What else you know? Dot-dot-dash.
Now add the old Caesar Shifting Cipher.
A dash of Latin learned at catechism,
in camera, sub rosa, in flagrante delicto.
All the signals made with flares,
all the signals made with hands:

Bravo: I'm discharging dangerous cargo,
India: I'm coming alongside,
Zulu: I require a tug, and
Uniform: You're running into danger.

Vulpecula, the little fox, is in ascension.
The rabbit comes back out of his hole.
No one's going to see what happens here.
We might as well be in India. Zulu.
Bravo. Bravo. Bravo.

BOONIES

Where we could be boys together. This region of want:
the campestrial flat. The adolescents roving across the plat.
        Come hither. He-of-the-hard would call me hither.

Sheer abdomen, sheer slickensides, the feldspar buttes
that mammillate the valley right where it needs to bust.

And I could kiss his tits and he could destroy me
        on the inflorescent slopes; in his darkest dingles;
upon the grassland's raffish plaits. And he could roll me
        in coyote brush: I who was banished to the barren
            could come back into his fold, and I
would let him lay me down on the cold, cold ground.

Clouds, above, lenticular, the spreading fundament,
        a glorious breech among the thunderheads
and in their midst, a great white heron magnifies
        the day. We'd keep together, he and I,
and we'd gain meaning from our boyage; we'd pursue
        each other through the crush of darkling rifts.
            Climb into each other's precipitous coombes.

Where would it end, this brush and bush, this brome
        and blazing star? There is always some new way
        to flex a limb and find its secret drupe.

        Not only the hope of nature; the nature of hope:

so long as culverts carry us, so long as we stay ripe
        to one another's lips, and welcoming to hands,
as long as we extend our spans, to tangle them,
                as spinning insects do their glistered floss.

This is not a time to think the trumpet vine is sullen.
Rather: the trumpet's bell is but a prelude.
        It says we all are beautiful at least once.
And, if you'd watch over me, we can be beautiful again.

LESSONS IN WOODWORKING

I'm in the clearing, now.
       He is my master carpenter;
and I, his joiner.
       We're putting up a front.
We reckon it's the front of a house,
       and that we'll live herein.
The raccoons haven't micturated
       yet upon the beams.
The pallid bats have not deported us
       back to the hot garage.
We've got our treehouse to erect.

"Pass me that piece there," he says,
       although he leans across
to grab the block himself, and where
       his arm just skims the knot
that is my shoulder, I come undone
       a moment, spilling tacks,
and there's a hammer in my pocket
       so uncomfortable
I have to pull it out and drop it
       in the grass. I will forget it
there. It's going to rust.

He'll take on more apprentices.
       I'll never learn to make
a miter joint. For one thing
       I'm just messy with the glue.
And though I pound the damned
       things down, my boards

come loose. My hinges stick.
        My only saving grace:
I am discreet. This time I'll meet
        him by the twilit wood. I'll
lift the rafters up. Just let him pound.

PUPIL

How is it that you hold such influence over me:
your practiced slouch, your porkpie hat at rakish angle,
commending the dumpling-shaped lump atop your pelvis—
as if we've one more thing to consider amidst
the striptease of all your stanzas and all your lines—
draws me down into the center of you: the prize peony,
so that I'm nothing more than an ant whose singular labor
is to gather the beading liquid inside you; bring it to light.

I have never written a true poem, it seems. Snatches
of my salacious dreams, sandwiched together all afternoon
at my desk, awaiting the dark visitation of The Word.
When you arrive, unfasten your notebook, and recite,
I am only a schoolboy with a schoolboy's hard mind.
You are the headmaster. Now you must master me.

ELEMENTS OF A CROSS-COUNTRY RUNNER

The horned lark favors a bare field.

Yellow nylon shorts, willing to glide
into crimps and gentled spans, as needed.

As needed, the singlet in scarlet,
which is also a towel, a headband,
a scrap to sop up excess perspiration.

The axillary funk, odor of the groin.

In the hacked terrain, his jerk and lurch.
The way the shrubbery scrapes his knees.

The rare spectator, who comes
to this inconspicuous stretch
between start and finish,

to attend his rise and stumble
across small heaves of shortgrass,

who hears the quick and slapping sound
as the runner propels his sleek body
forward, closing in.

MAGIC KINGDOM COME

Let in the needy, the glutinous,
the bald-headed children nearly posthumous.
Finish each thought with a sprinkle of pixie dust.
Hello, once formidable kingdom. Goodbye.

Usually, the days are crowded hot.
The line into tomorrow's weightless zone
takes considerable agency. Baby strollers bump
against one's anklebone. What a hangover one has.

Yes. One does.
Every choo-choo completes a similar circuit.
Zippedy bippity. Almost merry enough
to propel us into the firework-fretted fume.

How we do persist, ourselves and little urchins,
when every new attraction warns us off:
this is where the heart stops pumping.
This is where some big bad thing will get you

and shake the marrow down into your toes.
It were a barf. A blur. As pink as cotton candy.
Once more into the splash. A tiny choir shrieks
Please, Mr. Toad. The snug bar lifts too soon.

—for Vincent Guerra

SPACE JUNK

You are the sovereign who rides me; I am the ass.
We had made contact just beyond this sphere.
From among the planets, a tiny bit of space junk fell.

What would a cosmoplast look like if it were us?
Struck by its own discarded stages, which didn't burn up
on impact. That's why we need a more formal class

in matter. That's why physics. And that's why God
allowed us to make junk. He himself made junk of the void
and called them planets. A tiny bit of space. In space.

Alert the media that things are going to have to change.
For one thing, there'll be no trip up the Irrawaddy.
What would Jesus or Roger do? Take it up the Aswan

cataract as a suitable alternative. If love may be fallen into,
so might the meteor crater. So might gravity suck us
toward the great black hole in our own unheavenly crown.
Oh, infernal orbits. Even they will not keep us. Falling.

SPORTING LIFE

Love from someplace far afield dismayed me.
The pop fly, brusque rondure, dropped into my glove
for one easy out, for one chance to lead
with chin and shoulders high. The athletic slug

returned the sport of a dug-out's underhanded night
that picked at downy fuzz and nap on tarpaulin
or sedately sought among the clover for a cohort.
Fleet leaf, so brief. Not even worth the time it takes

to say, "the Stallions trounced us roundly on that turf."
He made clever with the puns on balls and strikes.
More clever still with brawn. He used his body as a club.

I nabbed his easy lob. The stands came scurrying down.
That queer joy of meteoric triumph shouldered me,
who spied his tinct, his quick red head hung down.

DYING IN A FALLOW

One by one appear the luminary pills
that flaw the blank black provinces of space.

Here lies my madder self, my nettled self,
spanning barbed goat grass, catchweed.

I might have assumed shearlings huddled
at the land's broad flexion. I might have expected
some creature to adhere in kind, to straddle
its mate, not for all the closeness of the moor,
but that it open, beyond one soul's duration.

& counted upon, certainly, the ambient gleam
of encroaching hamlets, now that their grainy noise
imprints the nerves of any living thing.

The self is such a bore with what it knows.
And maddening what a body can allow.

The weather has changed little,
but it has changed irrevocably.

Come, crude sun, and I will avert my gaze.
Hurl me over your shoulder.
Strewn dag. Cracked feed. Little lamb.

REACHING AROUND FOR YOU

Every invitation to lie back under concealing foliage
resembles in some way that earliest invitation
to wander the heady orchard in the long sharp afternoon.

Or to slip naked into the slough
with the wiry boy who peeled each apricot—
as if slightly uncertain how to partake of it—

and savored: dribbling it down his damp chest,
between his long clammy legs, and moistening
his whole delinquent body with pleasant juices.

The river rocks globular and slick,
the catfish with its wet dark skin,
and the afternoon's durable glassy eyes.

I do not mind you closing your own eyes, reclining.
Summoning the image of a lover put away.
Because virtue is hardly what either of us saved

from our separate, desperate beginnings. And because
stonefruit from a tin is almost as good as fresh,
when the spiteful frost arrives.

GOODBYE, MY FANCY

For years now, we've been criss-crossing
      this same largesse of valley.
It has provided for us, plenty. You've been
      my homoerotic sidekick, Bryan.
Excuse me. Ryan. There. You see?
I am promiscuous with even my own wit.
      & I can never keep you straight.

All the boys of recent memory
      have been like this: *accomplice,*
            adjutant, aide-de-camp.
I should just toss you my thesaurus.
      There are words for the kind
          of love we have,
though none of them quite suffice.
      Well. Why be verbose?
This is—to put it quite demotic—
         how we roll.

Whether stopping off in Stanislaus
      so I could nibble me some ribs,
or taking the backroad up to Dixon
      for your taste of hot tamale,
we've served each other well.
          Oh, we're a fine pair.
We also know exactly what to order.

Eventually, they kick us out
      of the Silver Dollar Saloon.
Buck up, my little buckaroo.
       Every Western ends this way:
          Sunset. Chaps.
The valley's just like San Francisco,
      but without so many kissers.

     The warbler has two notes
that he prefers from all his repertoire.
      But there are others he reserves
         for loftier joys, profound sadness,
as well as his most savage flights of fancy.

     These he also reserves for you.

HEREAFTER

Shorty the bouncer and frog-eyed Dixie did it
up in the buckbrush, on a bank of the Yuba.

The banks of the Yuba chirred, and pewees caught
a belly of mosquitoes; they made their bed.

He made her belly full and the gas tank empty
the night he drove her in his pity truck.

Bright was the moon and the name of the town
where he worked was Bryte, but he: not bright,

nor she, nor child, nor we who drove, hellions,
to Bryte and back, underage, bribing Shorty

with greenbacks and underage Dixie, so we could
fill our bellies with drink, drive back to Yuba City.

Town without Pity by Gene Pitney on the radio.
On the Radio by Donna Summer. *Summer in the City.*

Running on Empty. Hot Child in the City.
The Night They Drove Old Dixie Down.

MIDNIGHT COWBELL

One Night in a Lifetime

They must have been fine woodwrights,
joiners, masons, to build a tavern sculpted

After Dark

like flesh which wasn't wagyu beef; not prime,
in fact, it gave off a cattle company vibe.

Deputy of Love

Who laid a foundation for my ghost town,
then desecrated it as a form of public art.

Can't Slow Down

The venue was torched. & then the men.
Their hot bodies. The arsonist's revenge.

Shame

Audacious rooks will chase away a hawk
with notes this flat and this intense

All Night Thing

and reassemble with a cachinnating laugh.
I've never known this lurid bunch to quit.

You Should Be Dancing

DO THE HUSTLE

The true hustler had yet to be conceived, though his forebears,
lumbering freight trains, unlikely to couple, would find a way
to exert their will. Move in tight on that tight urethra.
Planning an accident, are we? You'll want the full insurance.

Elsewhere: the mess I made was to be nobody's boy.
One too many slow grooves with Aretha; one too many
pony kegs, and I'd have slipped it up with Joanie.
Fortunate: *Jaws* at the drive-in. Splattered sun visor.

Later some slick kid's mitts did rummage my drawers.
He had come for the shag. He tried to stay for the swag.
Tonight, I'm packing exuviated clothes in a FedEx box
like the stillborn infant his parents should have received

in time to save us all the grief of his living. And yes,
I too was a bastard. Doesn't mean nobody gets slapped.

ONCE AND FUTURE HOUSEBOY

Might have stranded you there
in the pumpkin dotted tillage of Wheatland or
the strawberry patch with your bum self sucking
every last drag off the cigarette you wore
like a piece of tacky jewelry piercing your upper lip.

But you are my little liebschen.
Refined as a packet of sugar I dump
into 8 ounces of coffee. I like it when you're sweet
enough to peel the gums away from my teeth.
I like when we're in misery together, accustomed
as we are to the sad café. Zip open that pouch of crystal
Let the cloying begin, my fine friend.

Do houseboys have houseflies? Something spews
white maggots still warm on the chaise, some
lone peacock preens in the sideyard, shakes
its feathers loose all over the portico roof.
I'm not pointing fingers. I know what happens:
you're feeling blasé; you go to the convenience store.
Six days later, you're disentangling from Reno,
pawning the only portable device you have
(which might just be your booty) and hoping
the locks weren't changed while you were away.

I should be glad to be rid of such a profligate.
But you're my evening lark. Up ahead, I am lost:
clouds smutching the drouthy stalks of corn.
My rake, unreliable as you are. Care for me awhile.

BACKDROP WITH SPLASHES OF CUM ON IT

Often I got stuck to the bottom of someone's shoe.
You've got a wad of toilet paper on your shoe,
his friends might observe. Well what do you know
about that? he'd say. But let's see how far this goes.

His turn. He felt a tickle in the back of his throat.
My turn. I went down easy as a good line of coke.
And so it went. He stripped me down
like a stick of good poplar used as a switch.

I got quite a bit done in those meetings.
Ten minutes here, ten minutes there . . .
You might use the mouth as you use the lavatory.
Now, that's industrious. In that case, go ahead.
Our love was lonely as a handjob and as frequent.
I'd try to tell him that in a better way if I could.
Usually not.
Those cigarettes will kill you man, he'd say.
And maybe they will. Come to think of it,
maybe they will. That's the way we talked.
We lived in an age of adolescence and irony.
Unless I'm thinking of another dude. That happens a lot.

How could you have anything but a vague memory
of a guy whose savoirfaire was delivered in the form of
I already told you that I think you're hot?

Well suddenly the present arrives, and it's a autopsy.
Maybe not that dramatic. How about the nerves

eroding. Slowly, the levee gives way.
Or maybe there's just a bad bout of hail.
          A surprising amount of hail, considering
it usually won't hail here. Wind catches you off-guard.
Upending lawn furnishings. Overwhelming the poultry.
          Yardbird's called a yard bird, you see,
                    on account of it don't fly.

When I see the flattened box of an out building
          lying in a rusty rhombus on the ground,
                    I think of so-and-so. Or whojamadoojy.
That's where I met him, the man who was it for now.
     The Luke who was my mark.
                    The Matt who was my john.
                    So many acts. xx

TRANSIT OF MERCURY

At the beginning,
      these were indistinct: the cortege
attending me my every astral night.

Before the sandy lake of light pollution
      sounded its coarse tongue
across the seductive bottom of the sky.

Now you're the one alluring planet
      I hope to reach, before we plunge
toward our separate gravitations.

Never having had affairs in order,
      I might not try to save you for the last.
Run, brief page, lest I should catch you.

I've got a heat-seeking missile for heartbreak.
      & so do you. If there's another side
of the sun, then you must hide there
      in less than your underclothes,
emitting every molecule of thermal funk.

      Thereby, create some other world that I
can be disclosed to, adamic, flayed of this sullied
      atmosphere. Promise to take away all my air,
astride me, astraddle, & hurl me to oblivion.

PLATELET COUNT DESCENDING

Which is why no biopsy.

Which is why no root canal.

Which is why the blood draw
made that simple stick
into a plum branch bruise.

I'm singing *Lady Sings the Blues.*

Panhandle Park is a bit attenuated,
too.

Easy to spot the blackbirds
in the sycamores,
as the branches denude.

What protects us
goes away. I get it now:

you probably still go bareback
as you were wont to then.

I needn't tell you check the mirror
once in a while.

I know you do.
And that you'll worry

if, like facts and blood,
you, too, begin to thin.

BACKSTAGE PASS

The rigging has come down again. Just last week
you fed on the free candy from the bank's candy dish.
Now you will be everywhere: Toronto, Ithaca,
Chicopee Falls. It's a bigger job than you expected.

So many components to the trap drum set: pedals,
wingnuts, hi-hat, snare. Be gentle with the heads. Yes,
that's what they're really called—check the package.

Just keep the bandmates happy, mister, just bring them
fudge, the Bud they asked for, the Amstel Light.

Whatever you have to do to keep yourself: in the back
of the bus, on a bumpy road, the scent of their underarms,
their bobbing heads, patting the back of your wrist.

Did you remember to pack extra sticks, the strings
and picks. Did you check. One, two. Did you check.

HAVING A RAMBUTAN WITH YOU

How implausible, this metropole:
its foreign-sounding streets,
imported golden privet, feral parrot,
camellias broad and red, the blushing fanny
of another naked runner flashing past.

And us, how we hang together.
In the leathery palms, a couple of fruit bats
wearied by all the domesticated pears,
the orchards blanding the razed inland,
the hybrid gist upon the branches in the barrens.

Delicate-scented polis drew us into its syrup,
with its heady buds and plump upthrusting fare.

Come, let's hunt for night's banana flower.

Such are the words you put in my mouth. Like *sport*
& *darkling wood*. Feels good to have them there.
In part, because you put them there. In part,
because we share a purblind foray in an urban patch.

City of such heretofore unknown delights,
we'd rather pull its little legs apart.
The furry pink button I wrestle you for
splits underneath like the backside of briefs.

The anus has started bleeding and will not stop.
That's one of six symptoms to worry about.
Symptoms of love? Perhaps.

Sometimes I tug you, too, with my happy teeth.

Sometimes, I forget to spit out all the seeds.

SUMMER OF MY BONE DENSITY TEST

The cottony skirts of the Matilija poppies
    will wax old quickly,
as the panniers of yesteryear have done.

Carbs will turn to sugars, and sugars to fats,
so even the most hopelessly beautiful man
    might soften and dwindle.

But isn't everything impossible to resist
what makes the living possible?
    And isn't there a Paradise
        in the foothills above Oroville.
Formerly unincorporated Poverty Ridge.
    You'll have to go with me sometime.

"Decent food despite remote location,"
Zagat might say, if Zagat cared to come
    crunch an apple some slow afternoon.

You'll get a choice of sides with every entrée.
    You'd love the sweet potato fries.
In which case, I recommend the salmon.

And the wild salmon will return to the brook.
    The hives will sit fat with honey.
The least shall be exalted. *Wow,* you'll think,
that could have been so much worse than it was.

I die a little all the time. And so do you.
    So do we all. It's the little things
like that that keep us from getting saturated
    in the panjuices of loneliness.

Otherwise, it's a cookout. A veritable meatfest.
We light the charcoal,
and the charcoal warms our little hearts.

We are practically at the bedroom door of disclosure.
You've got me in this paper dress,
just the way you've imagined.

I. Boy. Tell. Telephone. Prompt, please. Can't
tell, something something, delight.
Oh, I used to be so good at this.
Turn on one of your machines, then, Jacky boy.
Tell me how much I've got to lose.

THE GREAT UNREST

When I lie down I think, 'How long before I get up?'
The night drags on, and I toss and turn until dawn.
—Job 7:4

You'd think, bedraggled as I am by the illness of my age,
I'd be able to lounge a little.

That I'd shut out the noise, as others do,
and I would sigh and sleep.

Let me eat Tootsie Pops, I'd think. Let me lay in the moonlight
and grow the opposite of babyfat

Lie, I mean. Let me lie. I have had to wrestle with grammar
all my life. And what people call ideals.

I used to love ideals, but that wasn't cool. Plus there was money to be had.
And ass. Scads of ass.

Now I forget. The principal's your pal and not the principle.
At least I've retained that.

Give up your sleepless nights the man on TV said. Talking to me.
Like, how did he know?

I could have dozed through half a dozen shows and all the ads.
Even commercial noise

might have eventually been absorbed into my dreams.
It might have become my dreams.

But it's hard for me to lie still (lay still?) while I am getting fucked.
Sorry.

It's late and you been at me all night and I hadn't risen from it.
I was tired.

I'm even more tired.

But now I'm up.

ORCHARD IN JANUARY

Like a ramshackle crane fly,
the limbs, the rusted harrow.

Itinerant workers
with pruning hooks in tow.

She had that first child young.
They cut him out. Tilled

each day: short, clear, & cold.
A smattering of hailstones.

What's gone will be restored.

What grows grows in exile;
grows obdurate as any bough

that puts forth a good crop
and is sheared back, scanty

as the spring is populous.

ODE TO JOY

So many automobiles. It must be Friday night.
These are the golden eyes of catatonia of the valley.
Of. They are the lights of *of.* Their procession
       is a thread of yellow ore
across one bridge, across another
             confluence of rivers,
the ones that sometimes leave their beds
       and leave the shambled houses bare.
Well, even to belong in this congested state,
you have to spend a little bourbon on your nerves.
           They keep their low-beams on.
     It's part of *of,* a subset of *belong.*

Switching gears, to Slaughterhouse Rd.
       or Garden Hwy., or up to the junction,
or out to the boat ramp at cottonwood Star Bend.
Everyone's a little wet in the vee tonight,
       they're all getting sticky on the bucket seats.
In their humid zones, there are humid smells.
       They stopped for eats.
     Will everyone be fed this good in heaven?
Hey there, cowboy. Here's your Whopper.
All roads lead first to Burger King it seems.
Or Hal's Grubstake, home of the dudeburger.
This is one of those dreams that cause sleep-eating
      in which, as we float across a tiny bridge,
           our bodies, patty and bun, converge
and all we got to do is put the mustard on.
     The condiments of *of* can't stop your heart.

Of intimacy that flourished here, an outlaw,
just as the outlaws themselves had flourished

in the slapstick goldrush days, and men
who came from China without wives, and boys
who bundled together in the Okie jalopies, girls

finding their way together through the pass, and others
        leaving Mexico or Vietnam behind
                could reinvent the space they occupied.

Of teens, as teens must do, eating the potato nuggets
of cupidity, scheming them onto that hunting road
        of dirt, whereupon the greatest intimacy
                of *of* and *in* and *through* occurs.
Of all the random shots one young man takes,
        of hit-and-run trade, the hidden features
of men with boogie-woogie on their minds. Their cups
of catsup and other dipping sauces creating little o's
        of transparency in their suck-me-off jeans.
Of horrible missteps with fucked up chums.
                Of low desire. Of powerful urges.
        Of release by one's own adulterous hand.
Of and of and of the feeling.
                Of somebody else should drive.

Push Push in the Bush is the title of a dance hit,
        but it's just as easily a country song.
Out there, in the dark, they have found each other
like lightning bugs, despite the pesticides, despite
the blights that hit a town's periphery and stay.
There is a luminescence of all things.
        Of all things, which are of a place.
The place where they begin. Therefore, belong.

MISSIONARY MAN

We must bear away the body to another place.
—Oscar Wilde, *Salome*

Then said I, Here am I; send me.
—Isaiah 6:8

The product of poor radiography,
this one rectangular window through which
        the faintest of flowers might be seen.

As each plastered, vegetative eye awoke in traction,
        and sought to be dismissed
from the unreliable dispensary to which it was tied,
so too did I petition to be moved
        into any upper room that might have me.

Let the next who comes invite me so:
If night can take it, shall we thread it like a spider,
        glance around its unlit cistern
complecting our moonstruck strands
toward the vortices we've kept from thus exploring.

Let him knock with a promise of books. Good looks,
cut-away collar, skinny black tie.
        The pocket protector with his name engraved.

For the bandages were still to be unwound.
        Had I ever thought about being saved?
No. I had only ever thought about being spent.

And unmended in my bones,
I fostered such attraction to this ardent host,
        himself the aseptic argent lancet
brought to pierce me in my side.
        It was his first penetrating glance
that filled me with a sudden surge of blood,
        wrack, rent & bungle of my corpus.

Let me say I stank like the rim of hell in all my lust
and would have blushed at my own heat
        if not for the shameless eagerness in his eyes.
The world is full of lovely but tragic boys.
        Get me on the joy bus, I said.
Nobody ever really rides the joy bus.

He prepared a place for me in empty houses,
        received me in the shaded summer lawns,
wrapped in our own light jackets at the riverbottoms,
hid in manzanita clumps, the brake, the brittlefern,
        in the foyer of a Pentecostal church
where we took our gladness to spite the pious,
took the praise of God as an offering of our bodies,
        each of us crouched in the doorway in turn,
mouth to the vine, lips to the eucharist,
                flesh of my astonished flesh.

Jon, my elder; Jon, my boy.
        The body is dead to us: naughty, then gone.
Suffer me to kiss thy mouth, Jon; I will kiss thy mouth.

Let him be born of every ash that glows
          in the oil drums of winter parks.
Let lesions disappear, let brittle bones be knit.
Let the integrity of every artery be restored.
There is no God but that which visits us
          in skin and thew and pleasing face.
He offers up this body. By this body we are saved.

MASS FOR PENTECOST:
CANTICLE FOR BIRDS & WATERS

There is no cause to grieve among the living or the dead,
      so long as there is music in the air.

And where the water and the air divide, I'll take you there.
      The levee aureate with yellow thistles.
White moth, wasp and dragonfly.
           We could not wish unless it were on wings.
Give us our means and point us toward the sun.

Will the spirit come to us now in the pewter paten of the air,
      the fluted call of dabbler drakes, the deadpan honk
         of the white-fronted goose, the tule goose.
Tongues confused in the matchstick rushes.
     High, high the baldpate cries, and in the air,
and in the air, the red-winged blackbirds chase the damselflies.

Triumph over death with me. And we'll divide the air.

ACKNOWLEDGMENTS

Some of these poems first appeared in the following journals: *Alehouse, American Poetry Review, A Public Space, Barrow Street, Bayou, Boston Review, Catch Up, Cincinnati Review, Columbia Poetry Review, Court Green, Dritto, Field, Fourteen Hills, Granta, Gulf Coast, Hampden-Sydney Poetry Review, Harvard Advocate, Indiana Review, linebreak.org, Nashville Review, New England Review, Ninth Letter, NOÖ Journal, PEN Poetry Series, Pleiades, Ploughshares, Poetry, Poetry Northwest, Poetry.org (Poem-a-Day), Sonora Review, Southern California Review, Subtropics, The Journal, The Laurel Review, The Morning News, The New Republic, The Normal School, Tin House, TriQuarterly, Washington Square, Yale Review, Yalobusha Review* and *Zyzzyva*.

"Bugcatching at Twilight" appeared in *The Best American Poetry 2011* (Scribner, 2011), edited by Kevin Young.

"Landscape with Sections of Aqueduct" was reprinted in *Poetry Calendar 2010* (Alhambra Publishing, Belgium, 2009). "Pupil" was reprinted in *Poetry Calendar 2011* (Alhambra Publishing, Belgium, 2010).

"Landscape with Figures Partially Erased" was reprinted on *Poetry Daily*.

"Release the Sterile Moths" was reprinted on *Verse Daily*.

"Goodbye, My Fancy" was reprinted in *New California Writing: 2012* (Heyday Books, 2012).

"Do the Hustle" was produced by *Court Green* as a limited edition broadside.

"Orchard in January" was printed as a limited edition broadside by Bow & Arrow Press for Emory University's Raymond Danowski Poetry Library Reading Series.

"Cherry Blossoms in Spring," "College City Market, College City, CA," "Landscape with Temple, Mosque and Little Crosses," "The Kiwi Comes to Gridley, CA," "Do the Hustle," "The Fluffer Talks of Eternity," "Pupil," and "Almonds in Bloom" appeared in the chapbook *How Must Might Stain,* part of the Dory Reader Series from Small Anchor Press.

"Panic in the Year Zero" was delivered at the 220th Phi Beta Kappa Literary Exercises at Harvard University on 25 May 2010 and simultaneously printed in *Harvard Magazine* online and in the *Harvard Gazette.*

"The Great Unrest" was written for OccupyWriters.com. This poem is in the public domain and may be reprinted or distributed freely.

My thanks to the John Simon Guggenheim Foundation for a fellowship that greatly assisted in the completion of this book. Thanks to those who read and responded to portions of the manuscript while it was in progress: Jeff Shotts, Ryan Courtwright, Carol Ciavonne, Katie Ford, Sidney Wade, John Casteen, Kevin Prufer, J. Peter Moore, Jake Kelly, Austin Smith, Michael Theune, Peter Covino, Ryan Berg, Randall Mann, Cody Carvel, Susan Steinberg, John Beer, Matthew Siegel, Sho Sho Smith, Sam Witt, Rachel Zucker, Peter Kline, Luke Sykora, Christine Marshall, Andrew Rahal, Vincent Guerra, Joanna Klink, Luke Goebel, Walt Hunter, Louise Glück, Bruce Snider, Christopher Davis, David Trinidad, Max Andrews, and T. J. DiFrancesco.

And of invaluable service has been the assistance of Michael O'Donnell. Thanks, Mike.

D. A. POWELL is the author of five collections of poetry. His first three are published together in *Repast: Tea, Lunch, and Cocktails*. *Chronic* received the Kingsley Tufts Poetry Award, and *Useless Landscape, or A Guide for Boys* received the National Book Critics Circle Award. He lives in San Francisco.

Book design and composition by BookMobile Design & Digital Publisher Services, Minneapolis, Minnesota. Manufactured by Versa Press on acid-free 30 percent postconsumer wastepaper.

—